A STEP-BY-STEP BOOK ABOUT
CHAMELEONS

ROBERT ANDERSON

Photography by: George Dibley, Guido Dingerkus, John Dommens, Isabelle Francais, Michael Gilroy, Hansen, H. Lacey, Elaine Radford, Tidbits Studio.

Humorous drawings: Andrew Prendimano.

Distributed in the UNITED STATES by T.F.H. Publications, Inc., One T.F.H. Plaza, Neptune City, NJ 07753; in CANADA to the Pet Trade by H & L Pet Supplies Inc., 27 Kingston Crescent, Kitchener, Ontario N2B 2T6; Rolf C. Hagen Ltd., 3225 Sartelon Street, Montreal 382 Quebec; in CANADA to the Book Trade by Macmillan of Canada (A Division of Canada Publishing Corporation), 164 Commander Boulevard, Agincourt, Ontario M1S 3C7; in ENGLAND by T.F.H. Publications Limited, Cliveden House/Priors Way/Bray, Maidenhead, Berkshire SL6 2HP, England; in AUSTRALIA AND THE SOUTH PACIFIC by T.F.H. (Australia) Pty. Ltd., Box 149, Brookvale 2100 N.S.W., Australia; in NEW ZEALAND by Ross Haines & Son, Ltd., 82 D Elizabeth Knox Place, Panmure, Auckland, New Zealand; in the PHILIPPINES by Bio-Research, 5 Lippay Street, San Lorenzo Village, Makati Rizal; in SOUTH AFRICA by Multipet Pty. Ltd., Box 235 New Germany, South Africa 3620. Published by T.F.H. Publications, Inc. Manufactured in the United States of America by T.F.H. Publications, Inc.

CONTENTS

The purpose of this book is to introduce in a convenient non-technical format the fascinating facts about anoles, those little quick-change color artists commonly called "chameleons." It will also introduce their New and Old World relatives as well as their distant cousins, the true

INTRODUCTION

chameleons of the Old World from which their name "chameleon" was adopted.

The "Old World" pertains to the eastern part of the terrestrial globe, the Eastern Hemisphere, including Europe, Asia, Africa, and Australia. The "New World" pertains to the Western Hemisphere, the western half of the globe that includes North America and South America and all of the islands and surrounding waters.

The history of the only true North American species, the green or Carolina anole (American chameleon), is presented, as are the four species introduced into the United States from the West Indies—all of which now reside very comfortably in the State of Florida. All have been accepted and are now, for convenience, collectively referred to as American (chameleons) anoles. Their descriptions, habits, habitats, and distribution are accurately recorded.

The reader will notice that this writer makes no attempt to encourage any person to purchase a chameleon or any of its relatives for a pet. Only the true lover of nature and the very well informed should ever participate in any such endeavor that holds them responsible for the life of a living creature.

Facing page: Anoles are easy to care for; they are also fun and fascinating animals. Anoles make great pets and are an excellent introduction to the world of reptiles.

However, for those readers who are keeping or hope to keep any of these dainty little lizards as pets, there are suggestions on how to make a comfortable home for them, how to maintain them in a healthy condition, how and what to feed them, how to breed and raise a constant food supply for them throughout all seasons, and what other animals are eligible for sharing their home, as well as information about the hatching of their eggs and about their offspring. In return for this information, all this writer requests is that the reader will respect these little representatives of nature, harmless creatures with the attitude that their lives depend on you. All you have to do to maintain and enjoy an American chameleon is to treat it kindly, handle it gently, and let it feed from your hand. Only then will you enjoy and realize how quaint, docile, and friendly these little creatures really are.

All chameleons, or anoles, whatever you choose to call them, are very beneficial to all humankind; they feed on disease-carrying mosquitoes and flies and on many kinds of insects that destroy our food crops.

Iguana iguana is a distant relative of *Anolis*; both are of the family Iguanidae.

There are many species of *Anolis*; they comprise the largest group of iguanid lizards. Sunning on this rock in Grand Cayman is *Anolis conspersus*.

A BRIEF HISTORY OF ANOLES

These interesting little creatures belong to a genus of lizards called *Anolis* which in turn belongs to a large Reptilian order called Squamata that also includes the snakes. However, for convenience of classification, all lizards are placed in a special suborder, Sauria, and referred to as saurians. There are 20 families of lizards and more than 2800 species well distributed throughout the world.

The American (chameleons) anoles belong to the family Iguanidae, which is represented by more than 700 species. Anoles comprise the largest group of iguanid lizards (iguanas) and are quite a bit different from the true chameleons of the Old World but rival them in their ability to frequently change body colors.

The family Iguanidae descended from a group of ancient lizards that existed during the Triassic period, some 225 million years ago. However, lizards as we know them today were present during the Jurassic period, about 130 million years ago.

There are more than 300 named species and subspecies of *Anolis*. They make up the largest genus of reptiles in the Western Hemisphere. They are most abundant in the tropics. The green, or Carolina anole, (*Anolis carolinensis*) is the only species of *Anolis* that is native to the United States. However, four West Indian species now occupy many parts of Florida. They are most abundant in the southern and central parts of the state, including the Keys. Other species of *Anolis* occupy all of Mexico, Central America, and most of South America.

The most popular anole kept as a pet is the abundant green, or Carolina, species, commonly called the green anole or the American chameleon. It is safe to estimate that millions of these little anoles have been sold as pets to boys and girls all over the world. There was a time not too long ago when green

The most common anole is *Anolis carolinensis*, here seen perched upon a leaf. Known also as the American chameleon, the green anole has a long history as a pet in the Americas.

Introduction

Anolis carolinensis is also known as the Green Anole. Regardless of the species, all anoles love to climb. Include several safe climbing branches for your pet—they can be purchased at your local pet shop.

anoles were sold by vendors at circuses and carnivals as well as by pet and novelty shop owners throughout the world. Each lizard was usually equipped with a gold colored metal collar and a safety pin or clasp that could be secured to the new pet owner's lapel, shirt, or blouse. A long chain allowed the little creature to move about at will. However, because of the purchaser's lack of knowledge, more than 99 percent of the anoles succumbed to mishandling, starvation and/or dehydration within a few days.

History reveals that lizards of all kinds were an object of possession by the children of ancient tribes in many parts of the world. Many children born to the American Indians, past and present, at one time or another kept a lizard of some sort as a pet.

Today these little lizards are still being sold and harbored as pets by people all over the world. Most of them are enjoying a longer captive life than ever before because of the efforts of more educated pet shop owners and the writers and publishers who are interested enough to share their knowledge with a more educated keeper of pets.

SOME FASCINATING FACTS

Lizards belong to the suborder Sauria and are therefore referred to as saurians. They are far more abundant in number of individuals than any other reptile. Lizards are also more varied in form than any other group of reptiles. They range in size from the less than two inches in length gecko, *Sphaerodactylus cinereus*, to the 12-foot Komodo (monitor) Dragon, *Varanus komodoensis*. Their bodies are either covered by narrow rings (worm lizards) or scales. The skin usually lies in folds. Some have four legs, while those that are classified as worm lizards have two legs or no legs. The glass lizards, *Ophisaurus* sp., are without legs. The toes and fingers are variously modified. Climbers have broad pads that stick to smooth surfaces. Lizards of the desert areas have fringes along their toes that help them to move over loose sand. Some that do a lot of swimming have fringes or flaps on their toes. Slow-moving land dwellers have short fingers and toes. Most have claws. Some are long, while others may be short, slender, or stout. Tails will also vary among the species; there are long pointed tails, short pointed tails, and bluntly rounded, stumpy tails. Some lizards are capable of losing a portion of their tail to a predator and then regrowing the lost portion. The capturing of prey is most often done by the jaws that are usually equipped with sharp teeth. The gila monster, *Heloderma suspectum*, and the Mexican beaded lizard, *H. horridum*, depend on two rigid fangs located on the lower jaw to inject poisonous venom into their victims. Some lizards are, however, equipped with a long, blunt, sticky tongue to accomplish the capturing of insects. Food varies among the lizards. Some prefer a vegetable diet, while others eat insects and spiders—some may feed on the flesh of other animals, including carrion. Most lizards reproduce by laying eggs that are usually placed under moist soil or debris. Oth-

ers give birth to fully developed young. All reptiles are born in-dependent creatures and all are born cold-blooded animals. During the breeding season, male lizards will defend their home territories from other male lizards of the same species, but they will usually allow young males and females to enter.

In the wild, anoles feast on living insects which they catch within their quick jaws. For the health of your pet, try to include some live foods in its diet, avoid-ing of course any that have come into contact with insecticide.

TRUE CHAMELEONS

Family: Chamaeleonidae (*Chamaelo* sp.)

VARIETIES

The true chameleons are, without a doubt, the strangest of all lizards living today. They are found in Africa and Madagascar; one lives in Spain and Palestine, one in India and Ceylon, and two in Arabia. Both the longest, 2 feet (.61 m) in length, and the shortest, 1½ inches (4.0 cm) in length, live on the island of Madagascar. True chameleons prefer to live in trees, but some African species occasionally walk on the ground.

True chameleons are not only capable of changing colors that include the greens, yellows, reds, browns, white and black but they can also alter their pattern.

True chameleons walk with an odd, seemingly slow gait, moving their arms and legs one at a time. Their fingers and toes are fused, three on one side and two on the other. This adaptation forms grasping hands and feet that are used by these lizards for climbing among the trees and bushes.

True chameleons have turret-like eyes that are created by their eyelids which are fused with only a small hole in the center when their eyes are open. The hole moves as the eye moves. It is very interesting to watch a chameleon direct one eye cone or turret up and the other down or one to the front and the other to the extreme rear. Compared with the diameter of the orbit, the eyes are very small. This condition is caused by the surrounding skin or eyelids and allows the eyes an independent rolling movement and, consequently, great scope of vision.

Facing page: True Chameleons are of the Old World and distantly related to anoles—they are of a different family (Chamaeleonidae). They are interesting creatures with a very exotic appearance.

True chameleons have an extremely long tongue with a sticky enlargement at its tip. It is a tongue that is remarkably adapted for capturing insects, either resting or in flight. The tongue is actually a folded mechanism that is contained in a slender fluid-filled sac. When prey is sighted and its distance is gauged, a group of special muscles contracts around the fluid-filled sac and forces the tongue forward so quickly that the human eye can hardly follow its movement. The chameleon rarely ever misses its target. Another group of special muscles brings the tongue back and the insect is then swallowed.

Some true chameleons have long horns that project straight ahead at a slight upward angle.

The family Iguanidae contains a wide variety of species differing in appearance, size, and behavior; note the large and primitive appearance of *Iguana iguana* shown below.

The most common color of the anole at ease is a light green. Here an anole displays its climbing ability; because of its coloration we can assume that it feels free of danger.

ANOLES
Family: Iguanidae

Iguanas vary widely in size and appearance from a species a few inches long to heavy-bodied, five-foot-long reptiles. All are good swimmers; all have long, sharp claws; all are swift runners and excellent climbers. They are not aggressive lizards and rarely will attempt to bite unless provoked. The larger iguanas show irritation by lashing their tails. A full grown rhinoceros iguana can cause severe injuries with its tail.

Like most lizards, the tail of the iguana is easily broken off by the grasp from a predator or by an adversary during combat. Either way, it is an effective means of escape as it makes it possible by both confusing and eluding the enemy. The broken part will wriggle vigorously, snake-like, and the predator will stop long enough to capture and consume it. By

this time the tail's owner will be well out of sight and danger. The tail is regenerative, although a new tail is usually much shorter and without the original coloration.

In Central and South America, the green iguana is much sought after for food. For many years, and to this date, iguanas have been sold as pets by pet shops all over the world,

This is the green anole, the only *Anolis* species native to the United States. The relaxed stance exemplifies the docile nature of this reptile, as he is a popular choice for a pet.

with the green species being the most popular of all. They are hardy eaters and rather docile creatures. Some people allow a pet iguana to roam the house and treat them very much like a pet dog or cat. As a rule, the green iguanas are of a gentle nature, and with their bright colors they are attractive to those who enjoy having a showy reptile around the house.

Varieties

Caring for iguanas as pets is not an easy chore; food and drink are very important and should always be made available to the reptile. They cannot endure exposure to cold or dampness and must have spacious quarters. They should be provided with branches for climbing, plenty of heat and sunlight, and a shady retreat when needed.

The coloration of the American anoles is rather hard to describe because of its constant changing. The changing of colors among these lizards is an involuntary process that is brought about principally by temperature and light and their influence on the lizard's activity and also by anger, fear, and sleep. Anoles do not, as commonly believed, necessarily assume the color of their background. When describing these lizards an attempt will be made to describe their most common color as they would appear in a relaxed, natural environment.

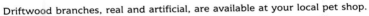

Driftwood branches, real and artificial, are available at your local pet shop.

THE GREEN ANOLE
Anolis carolinensis
(Carolina anole—American chameleon)

     Description: Average length of adult specimens varies from five to eight inches (13 to 20.3 cm). A specimen kept for study by this author was a male that presented the following dimensions:

Total length	7 ⅛ inches (18.10 cm)
Length of tail	5 inches (12.70 cm)
Length of head	¾ inch (1.91 cm)
Width of head	⁷⁄₁₆ inch (1.12 cm)
Length of hind limb	1 ⅝ inches (4.13 cm)

     A female is usually smaller and narrower with a more pointed head. Head is proportionately large and very distinct from the neck; the tail is long, round and slender. Formation of expanded, flattened, tiny scaled adhesive pads are present on four of the toes on each foot and enable this creature to traverse smooth vertical surfaces, including glass. The body is covered with minute scales, above and below. They are larger on the head and tail. On the top of the head is a ridge-like prominence (a shape that is rather similar to a javelin head) that points toward the nose. The skin of the body is somewhat loose and hangs in a fold at the throat; in male specimens, this fold is dilatable into a "dewlap." This dewlap can spread fan-like by swinging downward on a long flexible rod of cartilage attached near the chin. In some species, females will also have dewlaps, but those of the males are always larger and brighter in color. The dewlap is commonly referred to as a fan. The fan is a threatening or warning flag when predators or males of the same species approach. The fan of the green anole, when fully distended, displays a bright red skin between the scales which are separated by the distension.

Facing page: Although he may appear slightly awkward, the green anole is an avid climber able to scale the steep stump or driftwood branch.

In proportion to the reptile's size, the limbs are long, particularly the hind pair. They are more developed for jumping and climbing than for running over the ground.

Coloration: The most common colors are brown and green. Green is quite persistent in comparison with conditions, which greatly differ. When asleep, it is invariably a pale brown with a white belly. However, when badly frightened, the brown soon covers the entire body. At other times the lizard may be of a pale or rich green. This is most often the color of the side and dorsal areas when in the brightest hours of sunlight; the belly will be whitish, tinged with green. Some individuals of this particular species have changed to a somber gray or yellow color when exposed to cold temperatures.

The change of color is rapid. A dark brown individual turned a beautiful pale leaf-green within three minutes. During the change this particular specimen turned from brown to yellow, to slate-gray, and finally to green. During the change a peppering of whitish dots appeared over the dorsal area of the trunk. When spotting is present on a completed color change, it most often takes on the same coloration, sometimes a darker

The difference in color of these two Carolina anoles shows the possibility of different reactions to similar situations, pointing to the fact that anoles live with a degree of individuality.

A rarer species than *A. carolinensis*, *A. conspersus* is restricted to Grand Cayman Island.

shade, rarely a lighter one. False is the belief that any lizard—anoles and true chameleons included—will change its color according to the color of the object on which it is settled.

A recent purchase of four Carolina chameleons by my son proved to be very interesting. All four specimens selected were of various shades of green; but, in the couple of minutes that it took to place them in a small cardboard container, all had turned to brown in color. Upon opening the cover on the way home, all the lizards were of a dark green color. Once home, and the box carried to the terrarium and opened, all the lizards were again brown and remained so as they were being caught and placed into their new home. However, after an undisturbed half-hour all were a dark, rich green color once again. It showed that when frightened by movement and/or other interruptions the lizards turned brown. When observing the color changes, it was found that they were always the same: from light to dark brown, to slate-gray and yellow, to emerald green. American chameleons are truly fascinating pets.

Habits (in the wild): Strictly diurnal in habit; rising from its sleep as the sun rises. Resting often takes place on a

Anoles have been sold as pets for many years. Thanks to increased knowledge of their nutritional and environmental necessities, we can now keep anoles healthy and living in their captive environments for greater lengths of time.

horizontal twig of a shrub or low tree, usually well hidden among the leaves. The morning forage for food is prompted by its habit. A large flying insect is stalked very much in the same manner as a cat stalks a bird. Creeping forward, almost slinking, belly close to the branch; when close to the prey, body quivers, a sudden dash with jaws wide open, the victim is caught. Before the prey is swallowed the sharp little teeth masticate it. The choice of food is usually confined to insects and spiders. However, on some occasions anoles will eat the young of their own kind and those of other species of lizards. The green anole has also been observed feeding on newborns of the eastern ringneck snake.

Anoles are egg laying reptiles. One or two, sometimes three, oval-shaped, white, soft-shelled eggs are laid under decaying vegetation. Each egg measures about ¼ inch (.64 cm.) in length. Hatchlings measure slightly more than two inches (5.08 cm.) in length and are born independent animals.

BROWN ANOLE
Anolis sagrei
(Sagra's anole—Cuban anole)
Description: Average length is from 5 to 8¼ inches (13 to 21 cm.) in length. Body is stouter than that of the Carolina species and the tail is strongly compressed; scales are keeled dorsally and are large.

The bright blue dewlap of *Anolis conspersus* makes it a very attractive lizard. It is believed to be limited to Grand Cayman Island.

Varieties

Coloration: Usually uniform blackish or brown, paler below; longitudinal **streak on throat.** Throat fan, when extended, is a very brilliant orange-red or reddish brown, usually streaked with gray and bordered with yellow on the male. Coloration change is from pale, to intermediate, to dark brown. Some specimens may display six or more vertical rows of small round spots. The female has a very narrow stripe that runs the full length of the dorsal area and is flanked on each side by a row of dark brown "half-circles."

Habits: Although considered a tree anole, much of this creature's time is spent on the ground, whether sunning or foraging for insects and spiders. Reproduction is like that of the Carolina species.

Habitat: Wherever trees and brush are found within its range. It also frequents piles of debris, brush, and trees close to human dwellings. It can also be observed climbing about exterior walls and screens searching for insects and spiders. On chilly days it will not hesitate to enter the home.

Opposite and below: Anoles are abundant on the islands off the coast of Florida. Here are two different subspecies of *Anolis sagrei*. The below photo was taken in Bimini, Bahamas; the opposite in Grand Cayman.

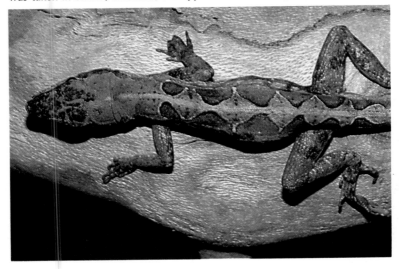

KNIGHT ANOLE
Anolis equestris

Description: Average length of adult specimens will vary from 12 to 19 inches (33.02 to 48.26 cm.). The female is always smaller. This is the largest of the genus *Anolis*. Everything about it is large when comparing it with others like the brown and green species.

Coloration: Most often with a background color of bright or dull green, but can change to dull grayish brown. There are two white or yellowish longitudinal lines that are prominently displayed, one on the shoulder and one that extends from just below the eye to the large ear opening. The throat is pastel pink.

Anolis equestris is a large anole that will range from 12 to 19 inches in length. Beware! A bite from this lizard may cause bleeding. It is best cared for by experienced hobbyists.

brown; some may possess green, but none are all green. Two longitudinal stripes are often present on each side of the body. Dark crossbands appear on the body, legs, and the base of the tail. The hint of a dorsal skin ridge is always present. Throat fan is pale or grayish yellow and may or may not have a pale orange central area. Female is always with a proportionately smaller head, a background color of orange-brown that is adorned with a mid-dorsal lighter stripe, and two yellowish spots on back of shoulders.

Habits and Habitat: Like those of the brown anole (*Anolis sagrei*).

BARK ANOLE
Anolis distichus

Description: Average length of an adult specimen varies from 3½ to 5 inches (9 to 12.7 cm.). A small anole whose

Some anoles, such as the Bark Anole (*Anolis distichus*), display a usual coloration of some shade of brown.

The common belief that anoles always assume the color of the object on which they rest is false—although one would question this after seeing the above photo.

snout-to-vent length is about 1¾ inches (4.45 cm.), rarely ever more than two inches (5.08 cm.).

Coloration: Often dark brown or gray with a changeable pattern which almost always consists of four dark chevrons on the back. Forelegs are lightly barred. Surface of the ventral area is sprinkled "dusky," more so at the sides of the throat fan. The top of the head has a straight line across the crown and two small spots at the back of the head. The tail is crossbanded. Throat fan is yellow and sometimes tinted with pale orange. When at complete rest or when asleep, the background color will vary from a very light gray to almost white.

Habits and Habitats: Same as those of other small local anoles.

DISPOSITION

The American (chameleon) anole is one of the most docile of all animals kept as pets. Some individuals will bite a finger of the hand that holds them, but this is strictly a defensive measure, their mouth being their only instrument of defense. When biting, one may describe them as having all the te-

nacity of a bulldog—they will hang on and will only release their hold when they are good and ready to do so or when they are physically removed. However, the teeth of all the American anoles are very minute in size and their jaws are rather weak for any real defensive biting of a human. Should this happen to you, please let it hang on for awhile or remove it by gently applying pressure to the sides of the jaws with very gentle fingers.

The males of the genus *Anolis* will almost always, upon mere sight of one another, engage in combat for the defense of females or territorial rights. Facing each other, fans are distended to their fullest, followed by some "head-bobbing" and "push-ups." Often times such antics will discourage one of the individuals before any fighting is done. It is usually the de-

Male anoles will almost always engage in a display of aggression at the sight of another male; combat often results from the attempt to guard territorial and mating rights.

...From T.F.H., the world's largest publisher of bird books,
a new bird magazine for birdkeepers all over the world...

CAGED BIRD HOBBYIST
IS FOR EVERYONE
WHO LOVES BIRDS.

CAGED BIRD HOBBYIST
IS PACKED WITH VALUABLE
INFORMATION SHOWING HOW
TO FEED, HOUSE, TRAIN AND CARE
FOR ALL TYPES OF BIRDS.

Subscribe right now so you don't miss a single copy!

SM-316

Being fascinating pets, anoles are also very photogenic; if you have a flair for photography and a love of reptiles, anoles may be the pet for you.

fender that will suddenly charge with mouth wide open and grasp any part of the intruder's anatomy that is available. The intruder will then apply a bite and both combatants will execute a few body rolls, twists, and shakes. No one really gets hurt; the weaker of the two or the most discouraged will make a dash for freedom. However, should the loser be grasped by the tail when making its exit, the tail remains behind with victor, who will, more often than not, consume it. The displaying of fans, push-ups, and head-bobbing, are also part of the male's courtship ritual.

Many anoles have the ability to voluntarily raise a dorsal ridge of skin that will usually extend from the top of the head to back and beyond the mid-portion of the tail. This dorsal ridge is most often at its fullest when these lizards are disturbed or excited.

THE ANOLE'S TAIL

All lizards have a tail. Some, like the anole's, are used as an instrument of balance for running or climbing or when perching on the branches of plants. Anoles are capable of

For their body size, anoles have a very long tail. The tail of this *Anolis conspersus* appears to be 150% of its body length.

Shedding is very common with anoles, especially with those kept in captivity—they can shed up to five or six times a year.

breaking their tail at a point where the tail is either grasped or struck by an intruder, making their escape possible. At the point of the break the muscles tighten around the blood vessels to prevent bleeding. A new tail, usually slightly different in shape, soon grows from the stump.

SHEDDING

The shedding of the dead outer layer of skin among reptiles is a common practice. This practice is more often done among captive specimens than by wild individuals. Unlike the snakes that usually shed their entire skin in one piece, lizards shed theirs in parts and may begin anywhere—the head, neck, trunk, tail, legs, or feet. Captive specimens have been known to shed as many as five to six times over the course of a year. Good shedding is always the sign of a healthy animal. If for some reason the shedding appears to be a slower process than usual, you may assist by holding the animal and with the aid of a cotton swab dipped in water soak the dead skin parts thoroughly. Then, carefully with your fingers or a pair of blunt-nosed tweezers, remove the straggled skin. All lizards have the habit of eating their cast-off skin. When shedding is completed, your pet will display a new skin of beauty, both in coloration and in pattern. It is at this time that you should take color pictures of your self-created terrarium, highlighted by your pets.

HOUSING

With a little work and creativity, the home for your anole can be a very attractive addition to your bedroom, den, or any other room in your home. This can be accomplished by setting up a temperate or semitropical habitat terrarium. All that is required, depending on how many anoles and plants you plan to have, is a 2-, 5-, or 10-gallon (7.57–18.93–37.85 liters) capacity glass fish tank (aquarium), low fern potted plants, small leaf climbing ivy, and a small branch. For the health of your pets and plants, a lighted aquarium cover will provide both light and security. Anoles are capable of climbing up the glass sides of the aquarium. If a lighted cover is too expensive, a glass or plexiglass cover may be used if laid flat across the top. However, this type of cover offers no ventilation, a very important factor for your plants and pets.

For those who have limited funds, or are pressed for space for a terrarium, or want to keep only one or two lizards as pets, they can purchase from the local pet shop a clear plastic container (about the size of a large shoebox) that comes with a clear plastic, snap-on lid. However, this type of container should always be placed in an area having a constant temperature of between 70° and 80°F (21° to 27°C). The reason for this is that no heating unit would be suitable, not even a small night-light. However, do keep a small thermometer in the container at all times. And last but not least, please remember for the sake of your pet's comfort, that even the smallest container must provide a hiding place for your pet as well as a branch on which it can climb or bask.

Facing page: House your pets in as large a container as possible, one that allows easy access to the keeper, is clean and sanitary, and contains many of the same things as the anole's natural habitat—such as this piece of driftwood. These materials can be easily acquired at your local pet shop.

Changes in temperature and humidity should be avoided as much as possible. Your pet and plants should be in sunlight for not more than one hour per day. Should the temperature show a sudden rise, remove the container immediately to another part of the room. Do not forget to turn off the light shortly after sundown, or when you retire for the night. However, this does not apply to a lighted heating unit.

CAUTION: Avoid excessive moisture! All plants should be watered once every two days and as close to the roots as possible—a basting syringe is ideal for this purpose. Watch for mold and unpleasant odors. Mold may prove dangerous if ingested by your pets. Mold can also destroy your plants. Soured soil gives off a sickening odor and should be replaced

Like the lounging iguana in the photo below, anoles also are essentially arboreal animals, and their housing units should be provided with articles, such as the Lizard Loft shown here, that allow the anoles to climb and bask upon. Photo courtesy of Dura Pro Products.

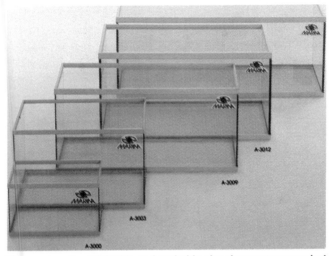

The most easily obtainable and probably also the most economical anole housing units of suitable size are the standard aquarium/terrarium tanks sold in pet shops. Such tanks are available in many different sizes and a number of different configurations. Photo courtesy of Rolf C. Hagen Corp.

immediately with fresh soil to prevent respiratory problems in both your pets and plants.

A homemade wooden cage with screened front and cover is not recommended as a suitable home for your anole. Unless the wood is treated with a waterproofing agent it will hold moisture and will eventually become permanently damp and moldy. As mentioned earlier, avoid excessive moisture in your anole's home. And again, mold can prove hazardous to the health of your pets and plants. Most importantly, untreated wood is hard to wash clean and will retain odors. Screening allows good ventilation but as a front for your cage it can spell doom for your pet. All reptiles have the habit of rubbing their nose against any transparent obstacle—a practice that most often causes them to rub off their nose and lip plates and invite

infection that will call for constant treatment with medication. Your anole will enjoy climbing about the screening but very often its extremely long toenails will get entangled in the fine mesh which can often cause a toe or leg to break during its attempt to free itself. So fragile are their extremities that you yourself can cause their breaking during the process of helping to remove your pet. Some anoles left hanging by their toenails have been known to die. Screening used as a cage cover should be placed at least ten inches (25.40 cm) above the highest object on the floor of the cage.

If you insist on having a cage constructed with untreated lumber, here are some tips that will help you to main-

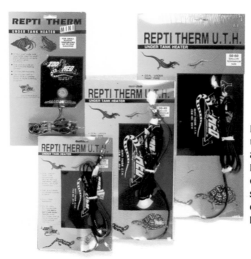

Heaters designed specifically for use with terrariums are widely available at pet shops. Inexpensive to operate because of their relatively low wattages, such heaters do an effective job of providing needed warmth. Photo courtesy of Zoo Med.

This outstanding head study vividly shows some of the anole's facial features, as for example: its hanging dewlap, sharp tiny teeth, and clear black eyes. It is *Anolis equestris*, the Knight Anole.

tain it. DO NOT wash it with water! Instead, sand the inside surfaces (sides, back, and floor) clean with a medium-grade sandpaper. When thoroughly sanded clean, wipe with a damp, not wet, cloth. Then wipe again with a cloth dampened with isopropyl alcohol, or spray with a disinfectant and dry thoroughly in the direct rays of the sun for at least one hour. The sun's radiation contains ultraviolet rays which kill most bacteria and molds, and the infrared rays supply warmth for drying. This treatment should be repeated at least once every 30 days or less. There are no guarantees, but it is the most that you can do. For a front for your cage, use double strength window glass that can be placed in ready-made anodized aluminum channels that do not corrode and are easy to clean. This material can be purchased in small lengths and then cut to desired lengths with a hacksaw.

Opposite : Whether lounging on a leaf or resting on a rock, all anoles enjoy and require a sun bath. For this reason, the appropriate lighting is essential in a terrarium. The ultraviolet rays, in moderate amounts, are beneficial to your pet's health.

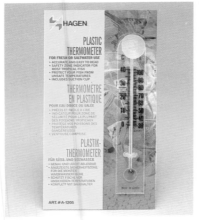

Thermometers designed for use with aquariums are equally suitable for use in monitoring the temperature in an anole terrarium. Such thermometers come in a number of different forms and are inexpensive but necessary items of equipment. Photo courtesy of Rolf C. Hagen Corp.

Units that conver the entire top of the terrarium keep dust and other airborne contaminants out of the terrarium in addition to serving as light-housing devices. Photo courtesy of Rolf C. Hagen Corp.

EQUIPMENT

Lighting

The light selected for your terrarium should, if at all possible, be of the fluorescent type similar to that supplied with a typical lighted aquarium cover. The advantage of fluorescent light is its cool burning factor. It will not interfere with your aquarium heating unit even if it is a 15-watt bulb.

Natural daylight contains ultraviolet and infrared rays that provide warmth and energy. However, especially during the summer months, keep a close watch on the thermometer. And as mentioned earlier, do not allow direct exposure to the sun for more than one hour a day, and then only if the container has adequate ventilation. NEVER place the container in the direct rays of the sun outdoors. It is best to place it indoors in front of a window that receives strong daylight, but no direct rays of the sun.

Housing

Incandescent light provides light and heat, but no energy that can be transmitted to your pet. Here again, keep an eye on the container's thermometer.

Fluorescent light is most ideal for inducing light in a terrarium. Light is provided without excessive heat. It is safe enough to be used throughout the summer months. Some varieties provide not only visible light but also some ultraviolet that is needed for the health of your pets.

Proper lighting in the terrarium is necessary for the well being of the anole. If environmental conditions are favorable, the reptile should respond in positive ways such as having a sound appetite.

The brown coloring of this anole indicates some sort of stress, as could be the case if the proper temperature is not maintained in the terrarium.

Housing

HEATING

As mentioned earlier, a thermometer placed in the terrarium is necessary in order to properly monitor the temperature. As you know, lizards are cold-blooded reptiles whose body temperature is controlled by the temperature of the room or terrarium in which they are kept. When body temperature drops, body function slows down and appetite decreases. And at the other extreme, too high a temperature will cause distress and sometimes convulsions that will kill the inhabitants. Temperatures between 75° to 80°F (24° to 30°C) are ideal. Do your best to maintain a constant humidity level between 60 to 80 percent.

Should a heating device be needed, always position it in a corner of the terrarium. A commercial unit is available at most pet shops, but a small 15- to 25-watt incandescent bulb

Heaters designed to duplicate the natural basking process of many reptiles, especially lizards and snakes, are available at pet shops and herpetological specialty stores. The units shown look like natural rocks and provide an even heat source. Photo courtesy of Zoo Med.

Communities of anoles can be kept if care is taken to ensure that all are of the same relative size, all receive enough food (no bullying takes place at feeding time), and plenty of room is given for each to have its place of peace if desired.

is adequate; if the terrarium is small or only a few degrees of temperature are needed, an ordinary night light unit will suffice. Do not allow any heating unit or commercial or electric bulb to touch the glass of the terrarium; in fact, it should be placed about one to two inches away from the glass sides; otherwise the glass itself will become a heating unit. When using any heating device, be sure to allow for some ventilation. Keep an eye on the thermometer, and your pets will be comfortable and healthy.

OTHER MATERIALS

All products involved may be purchased from your pet shop—plants should be obtained from a greenhouse. Begin by filling the bottom of the aquarium with small, clean gravel or pebbles to an even depth of about a ¾-inch (2.27 cm) for water drainage. Cover with a ¼-inch (.64 cm) layer of charcoal chips to help keep the soil sweet and odor free. Cover these chips with about one inch (2.54 cm) of loamy or sandy soil. Small, shallow-root plants may be bedded directly into the soil. However, for convenience in cleaning your terrarium it is best to use plants that are contained in small plastic pots that may be easily removed and replaced. When using potted plants, be sure to rest them directly on the charcoal or gravel layer.

Be sure to provide a retreat for your pets, like a piece of curved bark with its concave side down. Do not force this down into the soil. It is also important to provide a branch for climbing.

For a temporary or less expensive terrarium, a gallon jar, like a sun-tea jar, may be used with the same coverings and plants just described. Don't forget a branch for climbing purposes. For basic cleaning of your terrarium it is not necessary to remove your pets—such practice, too often, can upset them. Do not water potted plants while they are in the terrarium—remove them, water, and let them drain well before returning them to their proper places. A thorough cleaning of the terrarium every two weeks is sufficient. Be sure to clean the glass sides of it with a water dampened towel. Clean glass makes it more difficult for your anoles to climb on it.

Accessories that enhance the terrarium setting include scenes that can be attached to the back or sides of the tank; the scenes are available in a number of different forms. Photo courtesy of Creative Surprizes.

FEEDING

Anoles settle down quickly to life in a terrarium and will soon learn to take food from your fingers—quick, sudden movements should be avoided at all times. In captivity, mealworms and flies are the favorite foods; roaches, small crickets, and spiders will also be eaten. Mealworms should be placed in some kind of shallow container. Once your pet is trained to take food from your fingers, a small piece of raw ground beef may be offered as well as mashed fruits (apples, bananas, grapes and melons). Again, be sure that all are pre-mashed. In no way should your anoles be fed any moths that are coated with their own "protective" powder—anoles have been known to succumb to choking caused by such powders.

Some anole keepers will place a piece of ripe fruit, raw meat, or a container of syrup, or water heavily diluted with sugar to attract flies in the terrarium. If you choose to do this, remember that houseflies are disease carriers and should they lay their eggs on the meat, maggots will soon appear. This writer's suggestion is not to place anything in the terrarium to attract any insects. Any soft-bodied insect you catch may be placed in it and allowed to walk or fly about—your anole will catch just about anything that walks, flies, or crawls, except earthworms. Large anoles will eat small anoles. Allow about two dozen fly-sized insects a week per pet.

Facing page: For a healthy and alert anole, proper feeding is of primary importance. It is beneficial to include as many of the anole's natural foods as possible.

WATER

Anoles require plenty of water and when deprived they will quickly weaken and die. It is not necessary to add sugar to the drinking water and there is really no benefit in doing so. Their particular method of drinking water is to lap the drops of dew from vegetation. The terrarium plants should therefore be thoroughly sprinkled daily so that the lizards may be allowed to drink in their natural manner. A water dish is of little use. This writer has had anoles lap up drops of water from the tips of his fingers. Do not use any pesticides on your plants—it could dilute the water and make your pets sick or even cause their death.

BREEDING FOODS

Mealworms and sometimes wingless fruit flies may be obtained from your pet supply dealer all year 'round. During the summer months insects are abundant, and yours for the catching. However, during the winter months, food must be either purchased or, with very little effort on your part, can be bred and raised. Field crickets, the familiar black or brownish

Although mature beetles are often too large to feed to anoles, their larvae, known as mealworms, are a favorite and nutritious food of anoles; they are readily obtained from your pet supply dealer all year 'round. They should not, however, be the anole's exclusive food.

Crickets are both readily available and an excellent source of nutrition for the anole. This cricket has been dusted with a vitamin powder as an added source of nutrients for the healthy lizard.

crickets, are often abundant in meadows and fields and around dwellings or in gardens; search under debris in all of these areas. Collect about 50 individuals and place them in screen covered boxes with about one inch of clean soil, a flat stone or a piece of bark as a retreat, and a food dish with fresh, finely cut string beans or tomatoes or small pieces of white bread. Water is obtained from the food. Don't forget—field crickets sing both day and night.

Mealworms may be bred in a plastic or glass jar with about two inches of fresh soil on the bottom. Buy starter stock from your pet dealer, place it in a container, add a little bran flour and a chopped-up slice of raw apple and/or raw potato. Mealworms are larvae of beetles that will soon appear, breed and supply more mealworms, etc. The same procedure may be used to breed wingless fruit flies, but instead of soil, cover the bottom of the container with about ½-inch of a well mixed formula of equal parts of cooked grits, molasses or honey, and a small piece of yeast. After the substance is settled and level, crumble a sheet or two of notebook paper into a tight wad and place it on top of the mixture for the little creatures to crawl on. A good cover is a must or you will have these little flies

The *Anolis conspersus*, common only to the Cayman Islands, displays a magnificent royal blue dewlap as a territorial warning to oncoming predators who threaten its space or food supply.

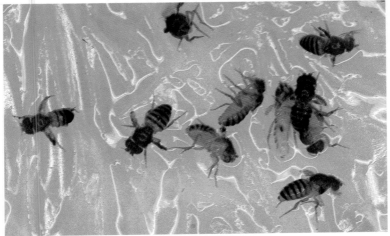

Wingless fruitflies can be bred in your home or conveniently purchased from your local pet shop.

throughout the house. A good barrier against escape can be made by folding a handkerchief into several layers and placing it over the top of the jar and securing it with a tight rubber-band. Be sure to offer your pets a variety of food, as too much of the same thing can discourage their appetite and also create digestive and excretory problems.

Crickets, which are readily available in the wild throughout the summer months, are a good supplement to your pet's diet.

TERRARIUM PARTNERS

It is safe to keep more than one anole in the same terrarium as long as they do not vary more than two inches (5.08 cm.) in length. A large anole will often eat a much smaller one. Males and females have been known to eat the young of their own kind as well as those of other species. Another reason for not mixing drastic size differences is that the smaller ones will always hide from the larger ones. It is good policy not to keep any anole that is less than four inches (10.16 cm.) in length. Larger individuals are much hardier in captivity, often feeding much better than the smaller ones.

Other kinds of animals, such as small tree frogs, may be kept in the same terrarium. These however need a little more moisture than your anoles. Other lizards of comparable size, both in length and in bulk, may be allowed to share the same terrarium. However, before placing any other kind of animal in with your pets, it is important to know the diet of the animal—mainly, that it does not feed on lizards, or any other animal that you are keeping in the terrarium.

Last but not least, male anoles have a habit of fighting one another. Do not worry; the fight is not to the death of either. At most, a portion of the tail of one or both may be broken off. If you wish to avoid these happenings, you will have to separate your pets. A male and a few females will usually do well together—more than one male may or may not work. A male usually breeds with but one mate per season, sometimes several seasons. Placing your males together often encourages

Facing page: Many frogs of the genus *Rana* are suitable partners for your anole, provided that neither is much larger than the other. Remember that frogs and anoles are both predators; if one can, it will eat the other.

fighting. However, a group of males has been known to settle down and accept one another. The best way to tell a female from a male is to place a small mirror in the terrarium—a male will usually display its fan in defiance of its reflected image. The fan of the male is always large and bright, while that of the female is small and dull. Another method is by hand check. Carefully pinch the skin-fold between your thumb and forefinger and slowly pull it downward. If it appears large and bright in color, it is a male.

Courtship and mating are observed rituals in healthy anoles. If mating is desired by the owner, it will be necessary to determine the sex of the anoles. Males typically have a larger dewlap that is spread in defiance, defense, and deterrence. It is often observable when a mirror is placed in front of the male anole.

Believed to be *Anolis* eggs, these small reptilian eggs were found during a photo shoot on Grand Cayman Island.

BREEDING

Should you be so fortunate as to have one of your female anoles lay eggs in the terrarium, remove them immediately and place them between moist paper toweling or, if available, moist humus or a small pile of decayed wood. Do not bury them deep, about ¼ to ⅜″ under the surface. Keep eggs very warm and slightly damp. An occasional fine spray of water may be added, but only to the surface covering. Eggs are oval in shape, white, soft, leathery shelled, and about ¼″ (.64 cm.) in length. If eggs are allowed to remain too dry or too wet for any long period of time they will not hatch. Eggs left to hatch in the terrarium may sooner or later be eaten by other lizards. And, should they hatch out, hatchlings will soon be devoured by their terrarium mates. Parent anoles have been known to eat their own eggs and young.

American chameleons have found a home in the hearts of many reptile fanciers around the world.

The following books by T.F.H. Publications are available at pet shops everywhere.

LIZARDS IN CAPTIVITY by Richard H. Wynne TFH PS-769

This book is a useful identification and maintenance guide for the amateur and professional herpetologist. Fourteen families of lizards placed as to distribution, habitat, description, cage needs and temperature range and other essential facts needed by the lizard collector are covered thoroughly. A glossary of terms, an excellent bibliography and a useful index of common names are additional values in this fascinating book. High school and up. *Hard cover, 5½" × 8½", 192 pages, 58 full-color photos, 67 black and white photos.*

SUGGESTED READING

THE COMPLETELY ILLUSTRATED ATLAS OF REPTILES AND AMPHIBIANS FOR THE TERRARIUM by Fritz Jürgen Obst, Dr. Klaus Richter, Dr. Udo Jacob TFH H-1102

Here is a truly comprehensive and beautiful volume covering all the reptiles and amphibians kept in terrariums plus virtually all the oddballs and rarities any hobbyist (or scientist, for that matter) is likely to ever see or want to know about. Illustrated in full color are hundreds of common and rare reptiles and amphibians, invertebrates, food animals, terrarium plants, environments, and diseases, with hundreds more black and white photos and line drawings. The alphabetical arrangement makes it easy to find information on almost any topic you can think of, and you can be sure the information is correct and up-to-date. *Hard cover, 8¼" × 12¼", 830 pages, 1,567 full-color photos, 381 drawings, and 168 black and white photos.*

Index